LONDON TRANSPORT BUSES

a black and white album

Mick Webber

Capital Transport

First published 2012

ISBN 978-1-85414-357-0

Published by Capital Transport Publishing
www.capitaltransport.com

Printed by 1010 Printing International Ltd

Introduction

This book aims to give a review of the main standard types, and many others, employed in London from 1933 until the loss of the Country area operations at the end of 1969. It does not aim to depict every variant of every class, but hopefully covers most, and in the main uses images not seen in print before. The feel of the past comes across very strongly in many views; rich in period dress, street furniture, and other vehicles of the day, and are therefore fascinating time capsules. Many archives have thousands of images, some of which may never see the light of day. In some cases, because of the way they are catalogued, they do not show up in regular searches, and appear in many obscure categories. I have trawled many of these, at agencies and libraries, borrowed from other collections, as well as digging out some of my own, and I hope that what follows will please. As any author will tell you, some of the pictures have proved impossible to attribute, and if any of the photographers are out there, please accept my apologies.

Compiling this volume has been immensely enjoyable, and many people have helped me with it. I must thank: Ken Blacker, Peter Horner, Ron Phillips, Jim Whiting, and Margaret McNicoll. Mark Dowd of Topfoto and Martina Oliver of Getty Images have also been extremely helpful, and thanks must also go to Anthony Roscoss of the London Transport Museum for letting me loose in the archives. The amount of material there is indeed a treasure trove that never ceases to amaze. I must also thank my sons John and David for help with the computer work, which is not my strong point. I sincerely hope that you will enjoy this trip through the decades.

Blackheath, January 2012

Mick Webber

Cover: The standardisation that London Transport had strived for came to fruition in the mid-fifties. The RT family double deck fleet and the RF single deckers are represented here side by side. The scene is Chislehurst, Gordon Arms, as RF 477 on the 227 from Bromley passes New Cross's terminating RT 2091 on route 228. The date is February 21st 1967. *Mick Webber*

Back cover STL 1352 is rounding Piccadilly Circus on the 19 in this late 1930s view and shows the distinctive rear end and upper deck emergency exit window of the majority of the STL class. The bus was built at Chiswick in May 1936. *Mick Webber collection*

Title page: The Q type single deckers came in three guises; centre entrance buses with bodies by BRCW, front entrance buses bodied by Park Royal and, last of all, Green Line coaches also bodied by Park Royal. All the class were in stock by January 1937. Q 194 is in Oxford Street and makes a bold statement when compared to NS 2246 in the background. The NS looks very outdated compared with all the STLs and LTs which are also in view, and the class as a whole has less than a year to run in London service. The date is December 8th 1936 and Q 194 is just four weeks old. No doubt some of the Christmas shoppers in the picture would enjoy a ride home on this modern vehicle. *Getty Images*

The newly formed London Passenger Transport Board inherited 2,202 of the NS type from the LGOC, LGCS and British in July 1933. Almost all were built at Chiswick using units supplied by AEC but some later ones were supplied as complete chassis by Associated Daimler. All had AEC 4-cylinder petrol engines and bodies were by the LGOC, Short Brothers, Brush or Ransomes, Sims & Jefferies. Most of the class had open top bodies and solid tyres from new. The Public Carriage Office did not allow covered tops on double deck buses when the class were first put into production, but this was changed in 1925. The majority were gradually converted to run on pneumatics and top covers were fitted, although London Transport took over 179 open toppers which remained as such. NS 1631 pulls into the middle of the road on route 67 travelling up from Wimbledon. It is scheduled to take 93 minutes to reach Stoke Newington. *Mick Webber collection*

Looking ancient with its solid tyres, NS 1864 was one of the class specially built for services through the Thames tunnels. The prototype entered service in April 1927 followed a year later by a batch of 24. They had tapered upper decks which were fitted with back to back seats down the centre of the vehicle, with longitudinal seats downstairs, and they had enclosed staircases. They were narrower than the standard NS and retained solid tyres until the end. The one exception to this was NS 2213 which received experimental pneumatic tyres with reinforced walls to resist wear on the steel lined kerbs in the tunnels. A supplementary batch of six was subsequently built with open staircases and normal seating arrangements, and NS 1864 was one of these. The tunnel routes were operated by Athol Street garage and NS 1864 on route 108B is featured here at Crystal Palace in LGOC days.

In June 1927 LS 1 entered service at Cricklewood garage and was the first six wheeled bus in the capital. The LGOC purchased twelve of these chassis from the Associated Daimler Company, all but LS 6 being double deckers, and fitted them with Chiswick built bodies. LS 1 and LS 2 originally had enclosed staircases but they were later rebuilt with outside stairs to conform to Metropolitan Police requirements. After operating on a number of services, all eleven double deckers were concentrated on route 16 from Cricklewood garage from 24th September 1930 onwards and remained on it until withdrawn in 1936/7. Whilst there, they had their seating reduced from 60 to 56 because of a weight restriction on the railway bridge in Kilburn High Road. LS 12 is featured in LGOC days, shortly after entering service in January 1929, running from Mortlake garage on the 33A, and LS 5, now with enclosed cab, is seen in London Transport days working from Cricklewood.
London Transport Museum/Alan B Cross

5

TD 37 is an example of the numerous Leyland Titans acquired by London Transport. This was one of a pair taken over from A G Summerskill Ltd and originally numbered L 88 before being changed to the TD series. It was a TD2 with Birch Brothers body and it remained in service until the last day of TD operation, 30th September 1939. It is at Manor Park working the 101 from Upton Park garage which was where all petrol engine Titans in the Central Bus fleet were based. *A D Packer*

An interesting rear view of LT 105 at Turnpike Lane station working from Potters Bar garage on route 29. LTs 1-150 were the last LGOC buses to be built with open staircases, and their open platform offered very little protection for the conductor. They looked very dated during the post war years alongside the emerging RT family buses. LT 105 was one of the very last in regular passenger service, being withdrawn in April 1949, but it afterwards spent a couple of months in the 'Special Events' fleet of almost time expired, obsolete double deckers used on such occasions as Epsom Races and Wimbledon tennis, being finally scrapped at the end of June of that year. *Don Thompson/LTPS*

LT 913 was built by the LGOC in December 1931 and was one of a batch of 450, all of which had entered service by February 1932. The last 111 to be produced had extensive route and destination displays including a roof mounted route number box at the front, and became known as the 'roof box' type. The scene is Friern Barnet terminus on September 27th 1948. The bus, which is working from Muswell Hill garage, has only eight months service left before withdrawal. *Don Thompson/ LTPS*

London Bridge station was London's first railway terminus and opened in 1836 with a route built upon brick arches all the way to Greenwich. It is pictured here in the last days of the Southern Railway before being nationalised in 1948. LT 972 was a February 1932 bus with a Bluebird style 60 seat LGOC body: it was fitted with an oil engine in 1934. It waits for the return trip to Shepherds Bush on the 17, its body showing signs of sagging. Withdrawal came in December 1948, the bus finishing its days at Hammersmith garage.

The impressive three sided forecourt to Edgware Station was built in 1924, but the north side was demolished in 1938 to make way for the planned extension of the Northern line to Bushey Heath. The war intervened, and the line was never built. ST 664 with an LGOC body was built in March 1931, and was one of many converted during the war to operate with gas trailers. The works for the new extension can be seen in the background, and two gentlemen prepare to ride off on their tandem. *Omnibus Society*

The first Waterloo bridge, then named the Strand Bridge, was opened in June 1817, and was a toll bridge until 1878. It wasn't too long before problems with subsidence were confirmed, and although steps were taken in 1882 to reinforce the structure, it became apparent that the bridge would have to be closed. This was done in 1924 and construction of a temporary one began. Demolition started in June 1934 and work began on the new bridge in 1937 but, because of delays during the war, it was not completed until 1944. The temporary structure with a 5 mph speed limit is pictured here on 31st October 1934, showing ST 648 on the right with a sister vehicle ST 580 both operating the shuttle service which ran from the Strand to Waterloo Station. *Topfoto*

In 1933, London Transport acquired ST 837-1027, which were previously operated by Thomas Tilling, the last five of which had been transferred from their operations in Brighton. These were AEC Regents with 52 seat bodies built by Tilling and Dodson, although it was not recorded which ones were fitted to which chassis. The layout of the three front upper deck windows made them easily distinguishable from all others in the class, and in pre war years they operated from the ex Tilling garages at Bromley, Catford and Croydon. Bromley's ST 974 is pictured here by Fox Photos man Reg Speller as it splashes round the roundabout on Blackheath on route 289A on 26th April 1934. This was a bi-furcation of the 289, which started at Bromley Common rather than Westerham. *Getty Images*

E G Hope, an independent operator in SW2 trading as Pembroke, handed two vehicles over to London Transport, one of which was this AEC Regent with 56-seat Birch body, new in May 1930. London Transport numbered it ST 1031 and re-seated it twice, to 52 in May 1934 and to 54 in September 1936. The driver had the luxury of a cab door, but the passengers had to suffer an outside staircase. Its final allocation was at Croydon and it is seen operating on route 75 in warm sunshine in the late thirties. It was delicensed at the end of September 1939, along with a large number of other STs, and was destroyed by enemy action whilst in store at Bull Yard, Peckham on September 7th 1940. *Mick Webber collection*

In May and June 1930, Short Brothers constructed six lowbridge bodies for the LGOC. Mounted on AEC Regent chassis, and numbered ST 136/40/41/57/62/63, they were operated by the National Omnibus & Transport Co on behalf of the LGOC. London Transport repainted them into country green, and ST 141 can be seen here on the 230. The new lowbridge fleet of RLH buses were on the horizon when this photograph was taken in 1950 and its service days were numbered. *Peter Mitchell*

The AEC Q type was a revolutionary new design, with side mounted engine and a full fronted body. Although over 200 of the single deck variety were to be purchased in various forms, an order was placed in 1933 for four of the double deck version. They were numbered Q 2-5, of which 2 and 3 were red, whilst 4 and 5 were green. The red buses had bodywork by Metro-Cammell with a front entrance forward of the front wheels, and the Country ones by Weymann built with centre entrances. Q 2 and 3 entered service at Harrow Weald on route 114 in July 1934, later moving to Willesden garage. Q 4 and 5 both began work at Leatherhead on route 406 in August 1934, and were transferred to Hertford to work the 310 in July and June 1938 respectively. They were joined by Q 2 and 3, which had also been moved to Leatherhead following the end of their work on Central routes in July 1937.
Q 3 is seen at Victoria station on the 52. *G.H.F. Atkins*

A curious addition to the fleet appeared in February 1937 in the shape of Q 188. This was the supposed forerunner of a fleet of double deck coaches for the Romford area Green Line routes. It was fitted with a Park Royal fifty-one seat body which had a centre doorway, and was the only member of the Q class to have a three axle layout. After negotiations with the Trades Unions, no agreement could be made and a spell in store at Reigate followed. The vehicle finally entered service at Hertford in June 1938, where it was used as a bus on route 310. It finally went to Grays with the other double deck Qs in 1939, where they were stored delicensed. It was finally sold in March 1946.
Capital Transport collection

Early in 1932 the Ministry of Transport extended the maximum permitted length for a two axle double deck bus from 25 to 26 feet. The LGOC took advantage of the situation by using the new, longer Regent chassis which culminated in the STL class, and by adopting a very upright front to the upper deck projecting well forward of the radiator, they managed to achieve a remarkable seating capacity of 60 as compared to just 49 on the ST. Fifty STLs were ordered and delivered between January and May 1933, and an order for a further fifty had been half completed by the time that the LPTB took control in July of that year. STL 1 is posed for the official photographer when new to General in January 1933. STL 157 was from the second batch, and is seen in the second view which, by the looks on some of the passengers, is posed for the camera. All had been withdrawn from service by January 1950.
London Transport Museum

Between October 1932 and June 1933, eighty STLs owned by the LGOC but operated by Thomas Tilling were delivered with Tilling's own 56-seat bodywork. They were initially operated from Tilling's garages at Bromley, Catford and Croydon and even in London Transport days never worked elsewhere with the exception of a few sent to the Country area to operate factory services from Hemel Hempstead garage at the end of 1946. Like the Tilling STs, the striking feature was the three front upper deck window layout. STL 96 is at Camden Town in the early days of the LPTB whose livery it now carries although the General name is shown. STL 115 is at Bromley on the 126 and is suffering from the body sag that plagued this class. They had all been withdrawn by October 1949. *Alan Cross*

Bromley South on a sunny March day in 1950 and STL 250 heads for Shoreditch on the 47. The ironmonger's shop on the left has a wide assortment of goods on display on the pavement and the corner shop advertises bottled ales and stout. STL 250 was an October 1933 delivery and was converted from petrol to diesel in August 1939. Its whole post-war operating career was spent allocated to Forest Gate garage, but on this occasion it is on loan to Dalston covering for an absent RT. Demoted to a trainer in August 1950 followed by a couple of weeks on the Chiswick skid patch in September 1951, STL 250's body was finally burnt in April 1952.
Allen T Smith/Alan Cross collection

London Transport took over five AEC Regents from Charles H Pickup in 1933, and they were sent to Croydon whilst still with their open top bodies. In 1934, LT decided to fit new top decks to these buses, and the result was rather untidy to say the very least. The original bodies were of six bay construction, but the new top decks were five bay, resulting in uneven spacing of the body pillars. They were eventually numbered STL 553-557, and STL 555 is working the 12 in the mid-thirties.
J.Higham, Alan Cross collection

A batch of eighty-five front entrance STLs was delivered in 1935. STL 984 arrived in April. In March 1938, the LT photographer was assigned to take this picture at the top of Botley Hill on the 403. The route was operated by STLs from Chelsham, Dunton Green and Leatherhead, STL 984 being from DG. *London Transport Musuem*

STL 1033 was another one of the batch of eighty-five front entrance buses built by the LPTB in 1935 for the Country area. They had 48-seat bodies, which were increased to 52 seats in 1939/40; they had oil engines from new. Eleven of the batch later received standard rear entrance bodies, and seven were fitted with Weymann front entrance bodies in 1947/8. *Mick Webber collection*

The railway bridge at Oxted on route 410 had a headroom of 14 feet, and therefore required new low height buses to replace the ageing PS types at Godstone. Twelve such vehicles had been ordered by London General Country Services; they were a standard Weymann 48 seat front entrance product with AEC Regent chassis, and were delivered to London Transport in April and May 1934. They did not receive fleet numbers at the time, and only when engineering responsibility passed from Reigate to Chiswick in February 1935 did they become STL 1044-1055. Their overall height was 13ft 1in and they were always known as 'Godstone STLs' although three were in fact allocated to Reigate when new. Bletchingly is the setting here.

The joys of the British Weather! A downpour has caused a flood beneath the railway bridge at the bottom of Kingston Hill, and the eyes on the adverts on the front of the STL seem to reflect a fear of water, as the driver ploughs through on his way to Kingston. The bus is one of the STL11 type built by the LPTB in 1936 with 56 seats. The trolleybus behind is Diddler No.50, which has just completed a clockwise trip around the Kingston Loop, and the driver is no doubt waiting for the water to settle down before attempting to move on. *Getty Images*

It is springtime in the late thirties, and STL 1156 from Tottenham garage waits at the stop at Moorgate, the driver looking behind to get the nod from the conductor. It is working a special railway replacement service to Finsbury Park station, and an Inspector leans against the litter bin as a passenger chats to the conductor. The bus carries an LPTB body built in January 1936. *Mick Webber collection*

In March and April 1937, the LPTB built forty STLs with bodywork designed for the Thames tunnel routes 82 and 108. They had slightly tapered bodies with arched roofs to accommodate the tight curves in both Blackwall and Rotherhithe tunnels: they were fitted with reinforced tyres to withstand the constant scrub on the steel kerbs. STL 1866 was one of these, and all were allocated to Athol Street, Poplar, near where the bus was photographed. This area has since been totally rebuilt to accommodate the Blackwall Tunnel approach road. These STLs were the last buses specially built for the tunnel, as when the RT family was being delivered it was discovered that these could pass through the tunnel without any special bodywork.

Looking like a scene from a Christmas card, this is very late snow on 26th April 1950 in Wickham Court Road, West Wickham. The telephone wires sag with the weight of the snow, and people at the stop are no doubt grateful to get on to STL 2505, Bromley bound on the 138. This Chiswick built 1938 bus moved from Bromley to Sutton, where it finished its days of service in June 1951, becoming a trainer until January 1955. *Topfoto*

The terms under which London Transport was set up required it to purchase a large proportion of its motor bus chassis from AEC. However this did not preclude the placing of a contract with Leyland for 100 Titans for delivery between March and July 1937 based on the TD4 chassis modified to suit London Transport requirements. London Transport was particularly anxious to compare the possible cost benefits of the Leyland 8.6 litre direct injection engine with those of the AEC's less powerful indirect injection 7.7 unit used in the STLs. London Transport was restricted by statute to building a maximum of 527 bodies a year at Chiswick, and as their requirements went beyond this figure they were able to order 100 of Leyland's own metal framed bodies for the new STD class. STL 1217 was sent to Leyland's factory as a template to help them adapt their standard product to suit. Most STDs had conventional crash gearboxes but the final ten were fitted with torque converters when new, although these were not successful and were removed at first overhaul. This view shows ten or more of the new buses on the production line at Leyland in February 1937. *BCVM*

The clean lines of the Leyland body are shown well in this view of STD 94 in the summer of 1937. This bus was one of the ten fitted with torque converters when new; known as 'gearless' buses, they had no clutch pedals. These ten all had 55 seats originally, but were reseated to 56 to conform with the rest of the class when the torque converters were removed, which in the case of STD 94 was in July 1939. It was withdrawn in May 1954. *G.H.F. Atkins*

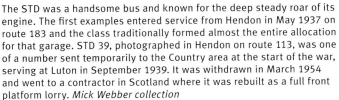

The STD was a handsome bus and known for the deep steady roar of its engine. The first examples entered service from Hendon in May 1937 on route 183 and the class traditionally formed almost the entire allocation for that garage. STD 39, photographed in Hendon on route 113, was one of a number sent temporarily to the Country area at the start of the war, serving at Luton in September 1939. It was withdrawn in March 1954 and went to a contractor in Scotland where it was rebuilt as a full front platform lorry. *Mick Webber collection*

STDs 65 and 42 can be seen here working from Hendon in 1937. The route operated from London Bridge Station to Hendon, with short workings to Golders Green, as can be seen here, the whole route being scheduled to take seventy-two minutes. *London Transport Museum*

STL 2311 was built in October 1937 with an LPTB 56-seat body. However, in June 1943 it was rebodied with a new lowbridge 53-seat Chiswick body, which was initially painted grey. Two other STLs from the same batch, 2291 and 2292, had also been so treated earlier that year. The bus is recorded at Bromley North Station on Godstone's route 410, waiting for the return trip to Reigate; it was the only one of its type to receive the plain 1950 livery. The bus was withdrawn in November 1952.

During the war London Transport was allocated 34 'unfrozen' AEC Regent chassis which always served in the Country area. Eighteen of these received existing bodies of various types but the remainder, including STL 2666, were fitted with new Chiswick built bodies. These were painted red when new but STL 2666 of February 1942 was like all the others in due course repainted green, in this case in May 1945. The whole batch retained their original bodies throughout their lives and this bus, here on the 455, remained at High Wycombe until its service days finished in July 1951. The body was scrapped but the chassis was stored and later became stores lorry 1015J in May 1955. *Denis Battams*

It is 13th July 1939, and the press and transport officials gather at the Aldwych to view a new bus and sample a ride to Hampstead. London Transport had started work on the design of a new standard bus for London back in 1937, and a prototype AEC Regent chassis was received in May 1938. The new 9.6 litre engine was not ready at this time, so an 8.8 litre unit was installed as a temporary measure. The Dodson body from ex City TD 111 was mounted on the chassis, and in disguise as ST 1140 it entered service from Hanwell garage on route 18C on 13th July 1938. By the end of the year, its new Chiswick built body was ready, and the bus returned to works for it to be fitted on 27th March 1939. The RT class was born, and RT 1 was the first of 151 of what are often known as 'pre war RTs'. The fleet of standardised buses that followed became the envy of transport organisations all over the World, with a family of nearly 7000 vehicles built from 1939 to 1942 and 1947 to 1954. London Transport's dream of standardisation was just around the corner. *Topfoto*

There were many losses to the fleet during the war; new buses were hard to come by, and were constructed to very strict utility designs. The Ministry of Supply would authorise construction of new vehicles, and the Ministry of War Transport had the power to decide who was to receive them. London Transport operated a total of 656 of these utility vehicles, entering service between October 1941 and April 1946. There were 11 Leylands of the STD class, 29 Bristols, 435 Guys and 181 Daimlers. The Guy vehicles were supplied with various body styles by Park Royal, Northern Coachbuilders, Weymann, Northern Counties, Duple and Massey. G 138 was a Weymann example, seen at Chiswick after overhaul in February 1951 with the wrong registration. It should be GXV794. The bus was delivered in March 1945. The class had all left service by August 1953. *John Gillham*

Facing page upper Representing the utility Bristols is B 10 of December 1945, featured at Wembley with an identical vehicle standing behind. B 10 was the first of a batch of twenty Duple bodied K6As. They joined an earlier delivery of utility Bristols, 'unfrozen' K5Gs B 1-9 with Park Royal bodies, and all 29 of the make spent their entire working lives at Hanwell (later renamed Southall) garage. All had been withdrawn by May 1953 and were sold for further use to various companies in the Tilling group. *Don Thompson, LTPS*

Facing page lower Like their Guy counterparts, the Daimler utilities came with a variety of body styles supplied by Park Royal, Duple and Brush. D 71 was a Brush example delivered in March 1945, and seen on route 32 with RT 139 bringing up the rear.

27

Duple built the body fitted to D 149, a January 1946 arrival, which was operating from Merton when photographed in Kensington after its first overhaul. The last of the class left London Transport service in January 1954. *F.G. Reynolds*

Above The pre-war STD class was extended to include the eleven utility Leylands, which were numbered STD 101-111. This view of STD 104 is at Leigham Court Road, Streatham, on 22nd February 1950. These buses were TD7s with Park Royal wooden framed bodies, and all spent their operational lives at Gillingham Street garage. The first was delivered in December 1941 and the other ten followed between May and August 1942. All had been withdrawn by May 1951. *Alan Cross*

Above right Between October and December 1946 London Transport placed in service 65 all-Leyland PD1 buses acquired as a stop-gap measure until the new post-war RTs were ready for delivery. They were 56-seaters numbered STD 112-176 which, like the pre-war STDs, carried standard Leyland metal framed bodies modified to suit London Transport standards except that they did not carry blind boxes at the rear. They were allocated when new to Croydon, Potters Bar, Loughton, Hanwell and Victoria but did not stay at the first two for long. STD 167 is working from Hanwell on the 92A on July 29th 1949 and like all of this batch was sold for further service in Yugoslavia. All had been withdrawn by March 1955. *Alan Cross*

London Transport had carried out a pay as you board experiment in August 1944. STL 1793 was used and adapted to incorporate a centre doorway. The exercise lasted only until March 1945, when the bus was withdrawn. The idea was not dead however, and later that year STL 2284 was the second vehicle to be so treated. The body from war damaged STL 1973 was used, and this was fitted with two doorways and a central staircase. The conductor was seated between the two doorways behind a small paydesk. The bus was allocated, like its predecessor, to Kingston, where it worked the 65 from November 13th 1945. It was transferred to the Country department in May 1946, where it operated on the 445 from Windsor. The problems encountered concerning poor timekeeping due to delays at stops eventually led to the bus being withdrawn in June of the same year, reverting to standard bus operation in September. *London Transport Museum*

In July 1945, the Ministry of War Transport granted London Transport a licence to purchase twenty new AEC Regents with standard provincial style bodywork by Weymann. Although they were not like any other STLs currently in stock, it seemed logical to number them in the same series, and so when they were delivered in January and February 1946 they became STL 2682-2701. They were all destined for the Country area, although the first three had been painted red, and all went to Watford. STL 2686 is pictured in Watford on the 332. *C Carter*

Facing page upper Having built 151 of the new RT buses taken into stock during the war years, London Transport was eager to resume the building programme after the hostilities. The bus was modified in a number of ways. The AEC A204 engine was used rather than the A185, and initially the bodywork contracts were to be shared by Park Royal and Weymann only. The main external differences between these and their 'pre war' counterparts were the omission of the rear roof mounted route number box and sloping base of the driver's offside cab window. Numerically the first, although beaten by Weymann RT 402 as being the first into service, was Park Royal bodied RT 152 delivered on 12th May 1947. The bus was sent to Leyton on the 23rd to start work on the 10. It is seen in Buckingham Palace Road in its first few days of service. It is interesting to note, that the bus kept its original body through three overhauls before being sold in 1958. *Julian Bowden/S.A.Newman collection*

Facing page lower RT 627 arrived at Chiswick from the Weymann factory on 24th August 1948, and was sent to operate from Leatherhead later that month. It remained at LH until its first overhaul in July 1952 and, keeping the same body, it returned in September for a further three and a half years. It waits here at Kingston on route 418 in the first few weeks of service. *Alan Cross*

RT 1050 was new to Leatherhead in March 1948. This Weymann bodied bus also returned to LH after its first overhaul, and is seen at work on the 408 travelling to Guildford by way of Croydon, Epsom and Leatherhead. This is how many would like to remember the Country RT. *Bill Godwin*

Experiments had been carried out in the past with double deck Green Line coaches. London General built one as LT 1137 in September 1931 and London Transport tried it with the six wheel Q 188 in February 1937, illustrated earlier. Neither was a success. After the war, the idea resurfaced. RT 97 had been damaged during the hostilities and was rebuilt at Chiswick to take part in the pay as you board experiments in 1946. When these trials were over, the bus returned to Chiswick to be completely rebuilt and fitted out as a luxury coach. It emerged as RTC 1. It had a sleek sloping bonnet, experimental seats filled with 'Dunlopillo', and fluorescent lighting in both saloons and behind the destination blinds. It entered service in April 1949, appearing on routes 715, 711, 705 and 704, but had been withdrawn by December of the same year and relegated to bus work from Leatherhead. It was finally withdrawn in March 1953, returning to Chiswick for development work before being sold in March 1955. *Bill Godwin*

In 1946 the Board could see that the production of the new RT family chassis could easily outstrip deliveries of new bodies from Park Royal and Weymann by 1948. It therefore became apparent that if the momentum was to be maintained, other body manufacturers would have to be found. After consultations, London Transport decided to award contracts to Cravens of Sheffield and Saunders Engineering at Beamauris, who were awarded orders for 120 and 250 respectively, the Saunders order later being increased to three hundred. The Cravens product, whilst being to the basic RT design, was radically different from all of the other RT bodies. It was of five bay construction rather than the standard four, and had a more upright front and curved back than the others. The first Cravens bodied bus was delivered in September 1948 and they were all in stock by April 1950. RT 1517 is working the 407 at Windsor after being painted green in May 1956. *Denis Battams/LCCTT*

London was plagued by smog in the early fifties. A combination of smoke and fog and very high levels of sulphur dioxide in the air made a deadly mixture, and in the worst case, between 4th and 8th December 1952, nearly four thousand people died as a result. The Clean Air Act of 1956 finally came to the rescue, and introduced restrictions regarding when, where, and which kind of fuel could be burnt. The smog conditions were often referred to as 'peasoupers'. Cravens bodied RT 1441 from Nunhead is crawling along on the 63 on December 6th 1952. *Topfoto*

The Saunders-built buses were much more like the standard RT in appearance, and proved very durable. The most obvious external difference being the offside lower deck route stencil holder set further back than on the other bodies. The first delivery came in December 1948, and all 300 were in stock by February 1951. The first 250 were delivered in the red with cream upper window surrounds livery, the final fifty in all-over red. RT 1343 stands at the terminus in Downe after its picturesque trip from Bromley North in the mid-fifties. *Peter Mitchell*

The other major player in the RT story was Leyland Motors. They were approached as early as 1946, and eventually were to build 1631 of their PD2/1 chassis with modifications to bring it to LT requirements and for it to be able to accept the standard RT body. An 8ft wide version was also planned, originally to be numbered RTL 1-500. The first 7ft 6in version was therefore numbered RTL 501, and was delivered in May 1948. By the time the production run started, it was decided to number the 8ft wide variant RTW 1-500, and so the next standard bus delivered was RTL 1. RTL 501 is seen in as delivered condition. *Park Royal Vehicles*

Some of the first RTL arrivals with Park Royal bodies were sent to Sidcup in December 1948, where they must have seemed light years away from the LT type that they replaced. RTL 32 was one of these, and quite what the driver was thinking here we shall never know, as double deckers had never been able to operate beneath the railway bridge in Station Road, Sidcup. It is 30th August 1949, and the roof of the bus can be seen at the rear, having been ripped clean off. It was sent to Chiswick for repair, and returned to service at Turnham Green in November. *Getty Images*

The legacy of World War Two is all around in this view at Farringdon in late 1950. RTL 1017 was a Park Royal bodied bus delivered to Chiswick in July 1950, and sent to Clapham on October 1st as part of stage one of the South London tram replacement programme. Route 45 required thirty-two buses on Mondays to Fridays between Farringdon and Battersea Bridge, to replace tram route 34. The route did not cross Battersea Bridge at the time, as it was closed for repairs. Park Royal RT 1877 waits behind on the 168. *Bill Godwin*

Below Between August 1949 and March 1951, four hundred and fifty RTLs were delivered with Metro-Cammell bodywork. These differed in a number of ways from the standard Weymann and Park Royal products, the most obvious external one being the central cream band being narrower than usual, but the most important difference was the body mounting. They were not interchangeable with other makes of body but were freely interchanged between chassis within their 'own' batch upon overhaul. Every effort was made to keep them within their original block of numbers RTL 551-1000, and only one instance occurred where this was not done, the resultant vehicle being numbered RTL 1005, with a standard chassis/Park Royal body combination being numbered RTL 626 to compensate. This is RTL 908, which is working stage 5 tram replacement route 184, at Brockley. *Bill Godwin*

Guy Motors had been very keen to get into the post-war market with London Transport, and in 1949 they offered a version of their Arab III chassis with a Meadows engine and air operated pre-select gearbox. It was stated that the chassis could be adapted to receive the standard RT body if required, but in this case a standard provincial style Guy body built on Park Royal framework was fitted. The vehicle was numbered G 436 and was delivered in November 1949. It first saw service from Old Kent Road garage on route 173 in January 1950, and subsequently passed to Nunhead and Enfield, being overhauled just once in January 1953. It appears here on the 173, standing on the forecourt of Peckham garage. It was sold in July 1955 and went on to further service in Yugoslavia later that year. *F.G. Reynolds*

Early in 1948 London Transport could see that there would be a situation arising where there would be an abundance of bodies and shortage of chassis for the new RT buses. This could not be allowed to happen and the remedy chosen was to renovate and adapt selected STL chassis to accept the new RT bodies as a temporary measure. The process began in October 1948 and the result was the SRT class, 160 being eventually completed. The venture was not a success however. The engines originally powering a lighter STL found it a struggle to propel the much heavier SRT, the braking was put under strain and the buses were not popular with drivers. SRT 70 had the chassis of STL 2572, with Park Royal body 4724. It entered service in September 1949 and was withdrawn in March 1954, its body being transferred to a new chassis, becoming RT 4487. *H.Luff*

Standard RTLs were arriving at a fast rate during 1948 and 1949, and RTL 75 with its Park Royal body was delivered to Chiswick on January 20th 1949. Its first allocation was at Hammersmith garage, later to be called Riverside to avoid confusion with the nearby Hammersmith trolleybus depot. It remained there until withdrawn for its first overhaul in December 1952, and is pictured on August 14th 1949, at work on route 72 at Malden Fountain. *Alan Cross*

RTWs were the first 8ft wide motor buses to run in the capital, but they were not initially permitted on inner London routes or along roads where trams were operating because of police views on the effects of the extra width on traffic conditions. In May 1950 however, trials were conducted on the routes converging on Notting Hill, and the 12, 17, 27A, 28, 31, 42, 52 and 88 were converted to RTW operation for a five day period. This was followed by another trial in Shaftesbury Avenue in June, with routes 14,19,22,38 and 38A, and the final one in Threadneedle Street from 3rd to 7th July with routes 6,8,22 and 60. The police had to reluctantly admit that there did not seem to be a problem, and eventually permission was granted to operate the buses on central London routes. RTW 420 is pictured on the 74 passing Brompton Cemetery, still sporting the restricted blind display. *G.H.F. Atkins*

Leyland's official photographer would not have had to wait too long to catch two RTWs together on route 11. The famous backdrop of St Paul's provided just the view required in Ludgate Hill, showing RTWs 294 and 96, both from Dalston, on what was then London's most famous route. RTW 294 had moved to Dalston after its first overhaul in February 1954, and RTW 96 likewise in July 1953. Both buses retained their original bodies. Note that both are turning short of their normal terminus at Shepherds Bush. A plant nursery has been set up on the bombed-out site on the left. *BCVM*

In 1950, the British Transport Commission offered London Transport a batch of twenty AEC Regent IIIs with standard Weymann lowbridge bodywork. They were buses originally intended for Midland General, but were now surplus to requirements. The lowbridge fleet was in need of replacement at the time, and therefore LT decided to accept the offer. The buses became RLH 1-20, and were delivered between May and July 1950 in green livery. A further batch of 56 was ordered and delivered in 1952, of which 23 were red. The prominent roof ventilators were omitted from the second batch and the bright chromium plated radiator shells were replaced by ones in polished aluminium. RLH 15 is seen at Weymann's works at Addlestone prior to delivery. *Mick Webber collection*

RLHs 21-76 featured the later AEC9613E chassis; 21-53 were painted green and the remainder red. The Central buses were operated from Merton, Hornchurch, Dalston and Harrow Weald, and it is one of the latter that is featured here. Route 230 worked from Northwick Park, where this view was taken, to Rayners Lane. *Mick Webber collection*

Bury Place in Bloomsbury is the setting of this wonderful view taken on New Year's Day 1952. Just pulling out of shot is Metro-Cammell bodied RTL 706 from Battersea on the 19, and following behind are two Saunders bodied RTs, 1294 from Holloway, new in December 1949, and 1314 from Forest Gate, new in February 1950. Two more unidentified RTLs are in view on the 19, and having just turned the corner is STD 167, one of the post-war 1946 buses, later sold for service in Yugoslavia. *Getty Images*

RT 3942 is embedded in a shop in the Edgware Road in May 1953 after an accident while working route 60 from Cricklewood. It is a Weymann bodied bus delivered in November 1950 and, after repair, it returned to work at Norbiton in June. *Capital Transport collection*

'I was doing the washing, when suddenly I heard this bang'. The lady seems somewhat surprised to see her unannounced visitor in the front garden, but then it does not happen every day. Quite what happened to cause Catford's RT 3072 to end up in this way whilst working the 124 is not known.
It is 1966, the house is on the Downham Estate, and the council would have to reinstate the lamp post. The bus was delicensed in March, and after repairs was sent on to Rye Lane in July to re-enter service. It was finally sold in February 1976.
Mick Webber collection

It is May 1950, and the staff at Weymann's factory in Addlestone have turned out to be photographed with RT 3201. They had seen many such buses at the factory before, but this green RT was a special one. It was the 1000th RT to emerge from the factory, and the management were clearly going to make the most of it, pictures appearing in the trade press at the time. The bus was delivered to Chiswick on 28th June, and commenced service at Staines on 1st July. The body and chassis combination remained as a unit through its first overhaul, when it returned to Staines until its second overhaul in December 1958. *Weymann*

Green Line double deck workings were not exclusively operated by the batch of RTs ordered for that purpose. Ordinary Country area buses often performed relief duties at busy periods as well as full scheduled journeys when required. RT 3725 was delivered in May 1953 and on 1st June it entered service from Windsor, its gleaming Weymann body looking resplendent in the sunshine as it performs a relief working on the 704. *John Fozard*

In August 1950, thirty-six Weymann bodied RTs entered service from Romford garage. These were RTs 3224-3259, and were built as Green Line vehicles to work the busy 721 and 722 services into London from Essex. In true Green Line tradition, they carried no external advertising and had a distinctive raised Green Line motif between decks. They were finished in standard Lincoln green but with a light green central band. They also worked the summer only 726. RT 3234 pauses on the 721 opposite a busy Romford Market. *Alan Cross*

On February 6th 1952, King George VI died at the age of 56. The new Queen, Elizabeth II, would have to wait until June 2nd 1953 for her Coronation, but when it came the whole country was decked out in flags and banners for days. London Transport had a major part to play in the celebrations, and Coronation route tours were conducted starting a week prior to the event. Twenty-one such tours, from different starting points, were arranged and were very well patronised, as were the Floodlighting tours, which began on June 3rd. Special arrangements were made on the day itself to terminate routes short of the area set aside for the procession, and extra vehicles were licensed to cope with the demand. Park Royal RT 1817 is seen in Old Bond Street on the 25, passing under one of the many decorations strung across London streets. *Topfoto*

The development work to produce the RT was considerable, and therefore AEC and the bodybuilders were keen to maximise sales by offering the vehicle to other operators. The take-up was very disappointing however, and the only sales outside London were two batches totalling forty buses to St Helens, all with Park Royal Bodywork, and a solitary vehicle to Coventry, bodied by Metro-Cammell to become the only Metro-Cammell bodied RT ever produced. The St Helens buses were delivered in 1950 and 1952 and the Coventry bus in 1951. *Capital Transport collection*

A great atmospheric shot of Holloway's Park Royal RT 1583. It is 7.17pm by the famous clock, one evening in September 1954, as a Vauxhall saloon is on the inside at the top of Whitehall, where the Brian Rix farce 'Dry Rot' is on at the Whitehall Theatre. This bus had its first overhaul in January of that year, and was to remain at Holloway until its next in August 1957. *G.H.F. Atkins*

Left According to the original caption for this photograph, this view in the Strand on 17th November 1953 was taken at midday! Another fog has descended on London, and all the lights are on, making it look like an evening scene. Merton's RT 857, picks up passengers outside the News Theatre. It is a 1948 Park Royal bus that was overhauled in October 1952, returning to service retaining its original body. *Topfoto*

Facing page Theatreland Shaftsbury Avenue on 29th September 1954. The Lyric is showing 'Hippo Dancing' by Robert Morley, and Noel Coward's 'After the Ball' is on at the Globe. Monty Fresco took this superb night shot for the Topical Press Agency, showing Putney Bridge garage's Park Royal RT 2706 on the 14 behind an Austin Devon and a Ford Popular. The bus was new to that garage in October 1951, and moved on to Chelverton Road and Abbey Wood before its first overhaul in September 1955. *Getty Images*

The idea for a next generation of bus for London had been raised as long ago as 1946. It was to be a chassisless vehicle of aluminium construction, it was to carry more passengers in more comfort, and it was to be lighter than its predecessors. AEC supplied the chassis units and engine, and London Transport built the 64-seat bodywork. After years of development, it was unveiled at the Commercial Motor Show in Earls Court on 24th September 1954, and after extensive tests and research, and an appearance on the South Bank in June 1955 at the Aluminium Exhibition, the 'Routemaster' was finally licensed for service. It was sent to Cricklewood garage to work route 2, which it did starting on Wednesday 8th February 1956 and is seen here on that dull day. It continued until August 8th, when it was withdrawn and sent to Chiswick for modifications, which included a new more conventional front grille. The bus recommenced service at Cricklewood in March 1957, being used on the 2 and 260, and was finally withdrawn from service in July 1959. It served as a training vehicle for many years until withdrawn in 1972, when it was sold to the Lockheed Brake Company. Fortunately, it was bought back by London Transport in July 1981 and is now in preservation. *PA Photos*

Not wishing to put all its eggs into one basket, London Transport included Leyland in the equation to produce the engines and running gear for two Routemaster prototypes. In a search for alternative body manufacturers, Weymann built RML 3 whilst the fourth prototype, a Green Line coach, was built by Eastern Coach Works and was numbered CRL 4. It is seen here setting out from Windsor on the long run to Tunbridge Wells, leaving a host of RTs behind both inside and outside the garage. *Peter Mitchell*

The production RMs began work in 1959 and, under the first trolleybus conversion to use the type, a new route was introduced between Poplar and Waterloo in November. RM 92 is seen setting off from the Waterloo terminus. *Peter Mitchell*

The need to produce lightweight vehicles to help with fuel economy had been a priority, and one which the Routemaster firmly embraced, but there was always room for improvement. With this in mind, London Transport decided to leave one of the new RMs unpainted, a practice already widespread with its Underground stock. This would reduce the overall weight of the bus by up to 3cwt and save on the high cost of repainting after each overhaul. RM 664 was the chosen vehicle and it entered service from Highgate on the 276 in July 1961. It visited a further ten garages until it was taken out of service in July 1965 and painted in the traditional red, re-entering service at New Cross in August. *Capital Transport collection*

After experiments over the years, London Transport finally ordered a batch of double deck coaches for Green Line services in 1962. One of the four Routemaster prototypes had been CRL 4, as we have seen, with Leyland running units and ECW bodywork. The production batch would revert to AEC power units with the usual Park Royal bodywork, but with 57 seats; they were numbered RMC 1453-1520, the first arriving on June 28th 1962. They were fitted with twin headlights, and inside had overhead luggage racks on both decks, with deeply upholstered seats and more leg room. RMC 1468 is at Hartford garage. *Peter Mitchell*

Facing page upper When production of the standard length Routemaster ceased in 1965, all further buses would be of the 30ft long variety. A batch of 24 four such vehicles had been produced in 1961 during the trolleybus conversion programme, and were created by inserting a 2ft 4in bay into the centre of a standard RM body. This added an extra eight seats, and the bus proved to be a success. The next 30ft buses to roll off the production line were a batch of 43 Green Line coaches. They were numbered RCL 2218-2260 and had 65-seat bodies very similar to the RMCs, commencing work at Romford, Grays, and Hertford. The whole batch was delivered in June and July 1965. RCL 2242 is on delivery from Park Royal in June 1965, and would start work from Romford garage. *Capital Transport*

Facing page lower An order for a further five hundred RMLs was placed in 1965. Fifty of these were for the Country area, and the rest were in red. RML 2606 arrived in April 1967. *Mick Webber collection*

The Country area RML is depicted by RML 2322 which was a November 1965 delivery to Northfleet, seen here on route 480 at Gravesend. The bus passed to London Country in January 1970, and was re-purchased by London Transport in August 1979. *Mick Webber collection*

Facing page upper In July 1964, authority was granted to order a batch of fifty Leyland Atlanteans with Park Royal 72-seat bodies for comparison trails with the RML, which began in November 1965. The Atlanteans, classified XA, started work at Chalk Farm garage on route 24. These buses were worked with a crew, as at the time the regulations did not allow double deck vehicles to be operated by one person. XAs 19 and 12 are seen at Pimlico, the southern terminus of the 24, on their first day in service. *Michael Beamish*

Facing page lower What might have been and, many argue, what should have been. The front entrance Routemaster was first discussed in 1964, and work began during 1965 with a great deal of secrecy. The completed vehicle was taken into stock on July 4th 1966, but did not appear in the trade press until December. Like any prototype, it had its problems. In August 1967, whilst working from Tottenham on route 76, it suffered a fire in the engine compartment, and having no opening windows, the bus quickly filled with smoke. It was returned to Chiswick, and opening windows were fitted, the forced air ventilation system being discarded. It returned to Tottenham in December where it continued as a crew bus, until going to Chiswick once more before being transferred to Croydon in December 1969 as a one-man vehicle, legislation having now been passed to allow this. It was used on the quiet 233 route, and is pictured at Roundshaw. After a repaint in June 1970, it returned to Croydon, and was later used on the busier 234 until January 1973, when after overhaul, it left for Potters Bar and route 284. It was delicensed following an accident in September 1976, and after repairs and a period in storage its final work was on the Round London Sightseeing tour starting in January 1978. It was finally withdrawn in February 1983 and handed over to the London Transport Museum. *Mick Webber collection*

In 1931 the LGOC rolled out the first single deck LT. This was LT 1001 which started work at Edgware. A further 198 were delivered before the year finished, all with 35-seat bodywork built at Chiswick and mounted on the AEC Renown chassis. LT 1188 was based at Bromley, and is seen leaving Penge terminus on route 227 in its later days after being fitted with a diesel engine from a redundant STL. The bus was withdrawn in December 1952. *Julian Bowden/S.A. Newman*

The single deck LTs were affectionately known as 'scooters', and the lack of a rear destination box on many of them is highlighted here, the only reference to its ultimate terminus being a wooden board. During the war many were temporarily re-seated from 35 down to 33 by placing the seats longitudinally to give room for 20 standing. This view shows LT 1187 leaving a stop in Sutton on December 8th 1934, and this bus was one of many renovated by Marshalls of Cambridge after the war. *LT Museum*

The AEC Regal chassis was the basis for the T class introduced by General in 1929. The first fifty arrived between December 1929 and July 1930, and had 30-seat Chiswick built bodies. T 30 entered service at Nunhead in December on route 621. The bus was built with a rear open platform but rebuilt in 1933 with a front entrance. *LT Museum*

Without doubt, the most unusual and futuristic looking single deck vehicle to enter the London fleet in the pre-war years was the AEC Q class. Q 1 had been built by the LGOC in 1932, using AEC's new chassis where the engine and radiator were mounted on the offside immediately behind the front wheels. The full-fronted vehicle was the forerunner of a class that eventually grew to 233. The prototype is pictured when in LT days, working from Reigate on the 460 in April 1937. *D.W.K. Jones*

As already shown, the new AEC Regal began service with the LGOC in 1929. Many variants entered service in the capital, with numerous bodybuilders. These, along with all Regals taken over by the board, were numbered in the T class. T 176 entered service with Green Line at Reigate in September 1930 and had 27-seat bodywork built by Hall Lewis. It is smartly turned out for Green Line route M in this posed view in the mid-thirties. It was converted into a service lorry by the Board in September 1940. *LT Museum*

T 271 entered service at Reigate in January 1931 with this 30-seat Duple body. It was one of the 250 coaches needed to operate the Green Line network at the time. Route D between Sevenoaks and Staines was operated by Dunton Green garage, and required four coaches daily. T 271 waits in traffic at Lewisham Duke of Cambridge, alongside a standard ST and a Tilling version. *Mick Webber collection*

Leyland Motors had introduced its Cub chassis in 1931, and London Transport had inherited one of these vehicles in 1933 when it took over the services of St Albans & District. This vehicle was later to become C 76 in the fleet and, pleased with the performance, the Board ordered another example in 1934. C 1 was delivered and fitted with a Chiswick built body, and was licensed on October 10th 1934, entering service at Hounslow garage. It can be seen here picking up passengers outside the garage on route 237 in November of that year. *BCVM*

The Board decided that the Cub was the ideal replacement for the assortment of small single deckers inherited, and further vehicles were purchased with 20-seater bodywork by both Short Brothers and Weymann. Ninety-six were delivered between March 1935 and May 1936, all with oil engines. C 69 was a Short Brothers example of August 1935, starting its life operating from Northfleet garage. Dartford is the location as people board the bus on route 450 bound for Gravesend. Note the garage code painted on the vehicle to the left of the nearside side light. *BCVM*

The BRCW version of the Q is represented here. London Transport's first order for the new Q single deck buses was for 100 for the Country department. The body contained 38 seats although this was altered to 35 in 1936 when a full width bulkhead was installed. Wartime alterations saw the seating altered again down to 32 to allow for more standing passengers, although this was restored to 35 after the war. This post-war view of Q 20 is at Redhill. The bus was withdrawn in May 1953. *J.H. Aston*

The vehicles classified as 9T9 were delivered between March and July 1936, and were the first Green Line coaches to be introduced by the LPTB. The fifty coaches had 30-seat Weymann bodywork, with an unusual front nearside wing and mudguard arrangement. T 423 was in the first batch to be received in March, and entered service at Crawley on route I to Watford. The whole batch were converted to ambulances in September 1939 and T 423 returned to passenger duties in March 1946, being sold in March 1952. *Alan Cross*

The next development in the T class was the 10T10, of which 266 were ordered, but this time with front entrance bodywork built by the LPTB at Chiswick. They arrived between January 1938 and March 1939. T 707 was a January 1939 delivery, and the caption on the rear of this post-war view states: 'Inspector John Turner, Leatherhead 1948'. Like the 9T9 coaches, they were all withdrawn and converted to ambulances in September 1939. T 707 was one of the ambulances surplus to requirements and was reconverted to a coach in November 1939. It was sold in November 1956. *Mick Webber collection*

In addition to the main class of Cubs, a further eight were supplied with Park Royal one-and-a-half-deck bodywork in June and July 1936. These were for use on the Inter Station service, based at Old Kent Road, and were painted in a blue, yellow and black livery. These were all fitted with petrol engines and C 108 is pictured when new. *Capital Transport collection*

The ageing private hire fleet was in need of replacement, and in 1937 twenty-four AEC Renown six wheel chassis with Weymann bodywork were ordered. They were delivered between September of that year and February 1938 and fitted with petrol engines taken from LT class double deckers, which were receiving new oil units. The bodies were fitted with sliding roofs, and luxury coach seats. The whole class operated from Old Kent Road garage from December 1937, and were all converted for ambulance use in September 1939. They had all been withdrawn by October 1952. LTC 11 is shown here when new. *Alan Cross*

Another new design after collaboration between London Transport and Leyland was the TF class, which incorporated the Tiger chassis with underfloor engine. The TF Green Line coaches were delivered between February and August 1939, numbered TF 14-88 and fitted with 34 seat LPTB bodies. They were all initially sent to Romford (RE) garage to operate the busy east London services, but like all other Green Line coaches, they were withdrawn on the outbreak of war and converted to ambulances. TF 31, seen at Epping, was converted back to a coach in March 1946, and re-commenced Green Line operation until May 1952, when it was downgraded to bus work until the end of its service life in May 1953. *C. Carter*

Leyland and London Transport joined forces again in 1937, and the result was a new version of the Cub chassis with the engine, gearbox and radiator mounted at the rear. Forty-nine of the CR class were built with Chiswick 20-seat front entrance bodies. The prototype CR 1 was delivered in December 1937, and the rest followed on between September 1939 and February 1940. CR 43 was one of the buses delivered in green livery and seen in Epsom. *Alan Cross*

In February 1953, a young Alan Cross travelled on route 494 from Oxted to East Grinstead. He took a series of views which included this charming scene at the Oxted terminus, where a mother, daughter and young baby share the bus with a cold looking young lady. The vehicle is CR 14 from East Grinstead garage, and is one of two to survive into preservation. *Alan Cross*

Two batches of the T class were delivered after the war. Fifty examples with 35-seat Weymann bodywork were received in 1946 and a further thirty bodied by Mann Egerton in 1948. The Weymann vehicles were a standard provincial style product, and were needed to give some breathing space until the new post-war LT designed vehicles would be ready. Norbiton's T 752 leaves RT 1222 behind at Kingston as it departs on the 264 for Hersham Green. *Mick Webber collection*

The Mann Egerton example of the post-war T is seen here. These were ordered for the Country department, and initial allocations were at Hemel Hempstead and Watford, Leavesden Road. One of the Hemel Hempstead batch, T 781, is shown at Watford on June 17th 1950. *J.H.Aston*

Like their AEC brothers in the T class, Leyland too supplied two batches of post war single deckers, classed TD. In 1946/47, thirty-one were supplied based on the Tiger PS1 chassis, with provincial style Weymann bodies identical to their T counterparts apart from their cab design, but with 33 seats. These were followed in 1948 by a batch of one hundred, but this time with Mann Egerton bodywork, again identical to that fitted to the post war Ts, the only difference being that the Ts were fitted with doors for the Country area, and the TDs for the Central area were not. The second batch were in stock by September 1949. The Weymann version is represented by TD 24. Kingston's TD 65 on route 218 is a Mann Egerton example.
Peter Mitchell, J.H.Aston

Very serious thought was given to the post-war replacement of the ageing pre-war single deck fleet. London Transport wanted to have one standard class that would sweep away the mix of types and simplify maintenance procedures, as they had done with the RT family double deckers. The AEC Regal IV was chosen as the chassis, and in 1950 the AEC demonstrator registered UMP227 was used at St Albans and Reigate for evaluation purposes. The bus had a Park Royal body and is working the 355 to Radlett. *Mick Webber collection*

The trails with UMP227 were a success, and an order for 700 vehicles was placed. They were to have Metro-Cammell bodywork, and would constitute four main variants, being private hire, Green Line coach, Central bus, and Country bus. The first twenty-five were the private hire version, and were 27ft 6ins long. The legal maximum length for a single deck vehicle was increased in 1950 to 30ft, too late to alter the order for the first twenty-five, although the remaining 675 were built to this new dimension. The private hire coaches were delivered in a smart green and grey livery, and were fitted with a public address system and glass observation windows along the roof sides. RF 20 and a sister vehicle are shown here. *F.G. Reynolds*

When the private hire RFs were ordered, fifteen 'long distance' coaches for the fleet were also placed on order. These were to form the RFW class, the W denoting 'wide' as they were 8ft in width rather than the standard RF of 7ft 6ins. They had the same basic chassis, but the 39 seat bodywork was built by Eastern Coachworks, and was finished like the RFs in green and grey. They too had curved glass roof lights, and featured four rear lights and extensive use of polished aluminium strip. They were all delivered in April and May 1951 and received two overhauls during their service life, keeping the original bodies. They had all been withdrawn by the end of 1964, ten of them being sold on to the Ceylon Transport Board. RFW 4 is shown when new, its first allocations being at Putney and Riverside, and RFW 6 shows off the nearside profile, its first home being at Romford.
London Transport Museum

The Green Line coach version of the RF first appeared in September 1951. These were the first 30ft length version of the class, and RF 26 entered service from Tunbridge Wells on October 1st. They were basically the same as the private hire version, but were fitted with luggage racks and the glass roof panels were omitted. Provision was made along each side of the roof for a route information board to be fitted. The batch was numbered RF 26-288. RF 265 was a May 1952 delivery, and is on route 712A from Dorking to Whipsnade Zoo. This was a summer only service that operated only in 1963 and 1964. The location is Oxford Street. *Peter Mitchell*

In March 1966, a scheme to revitalise the RF Green Line fleet was announced. RF 136 was renovated and unveiled sporting a new look, with twin headlights, a new curved windscreen and deep band of light green under the windows. The coach was transformed inside too, with new moquette and fluorescent lighting. It was deemed a success and a further 174 were treated, all being complete by July 1967. This view, at Northfleet garage in March 1967, illustrates the difference between the two styles, featuring RFs 655 and 179. *Mick Webber*

London suffered heavy rainfalls in September 1958 and in Sidcup two RFs are seen battling their way through the waters. RF 338 on route 228 is struggling to reach Eltham and shows the Central bus version, which was not fitted with platform doors, whilst Green Line RF 295 ploughs through on the 725 on its way to Gravesend. This had previously been RF 514 until renumbered in March 1956. *Mick Webber collection*

A Green Line RF on the 704 gets a helping hand near Sevenoaks on January 11th 1960. What chance of getting to Windsor? The Green Line and Country area RFs passed to London Country Bus Services on January 1st 1970 after the Transport Act of 1969 came into being. A total of 413 of them were inherited by the new company and RF 202 was the last to see service in July 1979, four months after the last Central area examples were withdrawn. *Topfoto*

The Country Bus version of the RF is represented here by RF 557. The folding doors can be seen as the bus heads for Woldingham while operating from Reigate in the early 1960s. It had been converted for one-man operation, as shown by the board on the front nearside of the vehicle.

In the early fifties, it was clear that a replacement would soon be required for the Cub one-man buses. London Transport opted to go to Guy Motors for the solution, and the Vixen with a Perkins oil engine was chosen. The bodybuilder was Eastern Coachworks, who incorporated several of their standard fittings, such as sliding vents, into a design that was nevertheless full of LT influence. It was a 26-seat vehicle and all examples were painted green for the Country area. Eighty-four were supplied between October 1953 and January 1954. Hertford bus station is the setting for GSs 73 and 18 on routes 388A and 388. *Michael Rooum*

In 1954, London Transport introduced the 800 series of route numbers for the Country area, the opening up of new services making demands that the 300-499 range could not fully cope with. Route 852 was a new local Crawley service that suited the GS very well, and GS 81 appears with a healthy load. The 26-seat capacity was the maximum permitted for one-man operation at that time. *Eric Surfleet*

London Transport had experience of the converted one-man RFs and GSs, but sometimes a lot of time was spent at stops as passengers getting off mingled with those trying to get on. In 1960, they decided to try out the AEC Reliance with a two-door Willowbrook body and three were added to an order that had already been placed by Grimsby-Cleethorpes Transport. These were duly delivered in August and September of that year, and formed the small RW class. They were tried out at Hemel Hempstead, St Albans, Hertford and Addlestone garages without a great deal of success. No more orders followed, although possibly some welcome knowledge was gained. They were sold on to Chesterfield Corporation in October 1963. RW 3 is seen at Hemel Hempstead. *Mick Webber collection*

On 28th November 1965, fourteen new Green Line coaches entered service. These were classified RC and were AEC Reliance vehicles with bodywork by Willowbrook to the BET standard design. Services commenced from Dunton Green and Windsor garages on route 705. They were soon to prove very unreliable however, mostly due to modifications specified to the standard Reliance by London Transport's engineers, and a very stormy two years ensued before they were replaced by RCLs. A period of assessment followed, and they were eventually used again on the 727 in May 1968. Problems persisted and they were soon withdrawn again, but later passed to London Country. RC 1 is recorded on the 705 when new in the grey livery in which they were delivered. They were later repainted into Lincoln green with light green relief. *Capital Transport*

On April 18th 1966, the new Red Arrow service 500 commenced. This was a flat-fare service between Victoria Station and Marble Arch. The new vehicles supplied were of the 'standee' type, with seats for 25 and space for 48 standing. There were fourteen of the new buses, classified XMS, which were AEC Swifts (Merlins to London Transport) with bodywork by Strachans. They were equipped with turnstile machines, passengers using sixpenny pieces to enter. Change-giving facilities were also provided.

The Country area was not immune to the introduction of the new wave of single deckers. AEC and MCW provided the new MB class of dual door buses with seats for 45 passengers. MB 110 is at Aldenham works, blinded up for the 430. It was one of the first batch of 33 for the Country area and displays the originally allocated registration mark of SMM110F. The bus was delivered after August 1968 and was therefore re-registered as VLW110G.
Bill Godwin

Commuta Mova!

London Transport have hit the bull's-eye with their Red Arrow service. The rapid transit, high density formula, which is used to move 5,000 commuters per vehicle per 5-day week, proves that AEC's rear engined bus design is right on target. More than 30 undertakings in the U.K. agree!

Swift: AH505 or AH691 underfloor diesel, 4 speed semi-automatic or fully automatic transmission. Wheelbases 16 ft. 6 in. and 18 ft. 6 in.

AEC

AEC LTD · SOUTHALL · MIDDLESEX
Telephone: 01-574 2424